Australian
BEACH
houses

Australian
BEACH
houses

living by the sea

For John Predny — who spent more time looking back at the coast than any of us.

Published by Lansdowne Publishing Pty Ltd
Level 1, 18 Argyle Street, Sydney NSW 2000, Australia

First published 1999
Copyright © 1999 foreword text: Philip Drew
Copyright © 1999 all other text: Lansdowne Publishing Pty Ltd
Copyright © 1999 photographs: Lansdowne Publishing Pty Ltd
and individual photographers as listed on page 190
Copyright © 1999 Lansdowne Publishing Pty Ltd

Text by Jenna Reed Burns
Foreword by Philip Drew

Commissioned by Deborah Nixon
Project Coordinator: Kate Merrifield
Copy Editor: Sue Wagner
Designer: Robyn Latimer
Production Manager: Sally Stokes

Set in Meta and Weiss on QuarkXPress
Printed in Singapore by Kyodo Printing Pte Ltd.

National Library of Australia Cataloguing-in-Publication Data:

Burns, Jenna Reed.

Australian beach houses: living by the sea.
Includes index.

ISBN 1 86302 656 8

1. Vacation homes – Australia – Designs and plans.2
Vacation homes – Australia. I. Title.

690.8720994

foreword

The beach house has an interesting history and has long enjoyed fluctuating fortunes. Its antecedents can be traced back to the early 1st century AD when imaginative *villae marittimae* (marine villas) were the subject of architectural experiment. Wealthy Roman upper-class citizens, including such prominent figures as Julius Caesar and Pompey, ringed the Bay of Naples with elaborate seaside retreats.

But it wasn't until the 19th century that Romanticism brought a rush to the seaside with its notions of escaping in nature — a romantic reaction that remains at the core of the beach house's appeal today.

In Australia, the great push to populate the inland which consumed the 19th-century population was in full retreat by the 1990s. Before the 1960s, it was the poor who lived near the beach because it was cheap and not considered desirable. Many people even moved onto the beach during the Depression, using cheap and ordinary materials in the construction of their beach houses. The unpretentiousness, lack of style, and unconcern for ostentation and display in early beach houses originated from this tradition of cheap living.

After 1960 the development of a surfing culture gave many people a reason to be near the sea. This new class, who derived aesthetic pleasure from the sea, joined the fishermen who made their livings from it. At first it was the middle-class weekender movement, who built beach houses which were unconcerned with notions of class and wealth. That all changed when the developer juggernaut took over the seaside with beachfront strips of hotels, specialty shops and marina housing. Sprawling coastal resorts such as Surfers Paradise are the result and the humble beach house was the victim.

Seaside land with water views is now seen as a secure investment and ordinary folk are relegated to the back blocks as beach frontage land becomes more expensive. The humble beach house has been succeeded by elaborate and architecturally exquisite marine villas owned by the wealthy.

However, the reasons for wanting to be beside the sea are the same, no matter what style of beach house one can afford. The sea is a place of retirement. When people attempt to explain the appeal of the beach house it is in terms of a retreat, a means of getting away from the stresses of work and city life. Turning away from society and towards the sea offers a way of recharging our batteries.

At the beach house we can draw closer to our inner selves. It offers a special form of privacy, a chance to commune with nature, a quiet place characterised by sets of simple pleasures — talking around the barbeque, walking, fishing, surfing — elemental experiences that draw us back to a more primitive, simpler, less-complex type of existence.

In that sense, the beach house is a branch of religious architecture. It is where we can come to terms with our selves, with our own lives, with nature, with life and earth and eternity. The eschewing of form, reducing everything to all but the most basic conveniences, its openess and lack of internal barriers or compartments is almost a psychological model of our own nakedness, an admission of vulnerability and smallness before nature.

It is tempting to call the beach house a form of white dreaming. In a secular society that has lost its traditional guideposts and sources of belief and spiritual comfort, the beach house has become a spiritual retreat. And in its way, the casual disorder found in most beach houses paints a picture of the Australian soul.

PHILIP DREW

contents

introduction

In his book *Land's Edge*, Tim Winton explores the reasons why his strongest childhood memories are of summer holidays, of days spent on the local city beach in Perth or up at a holiday shack near Geraldton. He finds it impossible to remember winter and strains to recognise himself on rare family slide nights as a youngster dressed in a glistening yellow raincoat. For Winton, childhood was one long summer of bare feet, suntanned skin and a peeling nose.

It is likely to be the same for many Australians. Why? Most urban dwellers know that they have lived two lives: winter in the suburbs, summer on the beach. The reason Winton gives for his selective memory is that he simply lived the latter with 'more passion. I recognised that life, embraced it and made it my own.'

The sensuality of the beach is what we all respond to. It makes us acutely aware of our physical being, which is why seaside memories are so deeply ingrained. All of our senses are heightened by the beach. We can easily recall the taste of salt on our tongues, the crunch of dry sand underfoot, the crash of waves on the shore, the smell of seaweed washed up on the high tide, and the sight of the ever-changing colour of the sea depending on the time of day — anything from soft milky green, to steel grey or deep royal blue.

Australians are essentially a coastal people. More than 70 per cent of the population lives within coo-ee of the beach, with the majority clustering along the eastern seaboard, from Victoria all the way up to and along the Queensland coast. To the west there are a couple of smaller outlying pockets: on the south-west coast of Western Australia, centred on Perth and Fremantle, and

another between the two peninsulas which enclose the Gulf of St Vincent — the city of Adelaide. All of our major cities are near the water, and most of us choose to holiday near it as well, especially over the long Christmas summer holidays.

The coastal nature of white Australians can be traced back to the first Europeans who settled here. By necessity they stayed near the coast as supplies were delivered by sea. But they also remained close to the water because it was a known, unlike the landscape behind them which they perceived as alien, harsh and unforgiving. They dealt with this fear by turning their backs on the land and facing out to sea, towards distant homelands.

The importance of the sea and the beach to us as a people is reflected in our culture — in art, literature, photography and film the beach is the stage on which most of life's dramas are played out — because it's like that in real life. Author Robert Drewe maintains that almost every Australian rite of passage happens either on the beach, behind in the dunes or in the beach house nearby. The seafront is where we establish important friendships and become sensual and often also sexual beings.

The beach house, therefore, has a special place in our collective consciousness, imbued with all of these memories. Mention it to people and many smile wistfully, immediately cast back to childhood and adolescent memories. To own a beach house is a dream that most Australians cling to. And the day they retire, you won't see them for dust as they head towards the coast where they will settle in some beachside suburb or town, spending their days fishing, beachcombing and gazing out to sea.

The sea draws it to us for rest and relaxation. It's a place where we can empty our minds and restore our spirits. Onshore breezes — temperate in summer, wild in winter — blow away urban anxieties. Perhaps the endlessness of the horizon is what rejuvenates us, or the enormous reserve of restless energy that is the sea. As Winton says, looking out at the sea is as close to infinity as we'll ever get. Its vastness puts human existence and concerns into perspective.

When we venture up or down the coast we temporarily turn our backs on society and all of its constraints and mores. We escape, and the beach house becomes a sanctuary. It encourages us to kick off our shoes and be ourselves. We become more attuned to nature and the landscape, to the changing seasons. Perhaps, as architect Lindsay Clare says, spending time at the beach house allows us to become more Australian.

Beach house architecture has changed over the decades and this book charts its evolution, while celebrating its various styles. What began as a scattering of humble little shacks, often knocked together from secondhand materials by untrained hands and added to over time to create ramshackle dwellings of considerable charm, has evolved into its own genre. As we at last begin to feel more comfortable in this country, we are opening up our houses to the landscape, rather than wanting them to hem us in securely. The materials which clad beach houses are now often left unpainted, allowing them to mellow and age gracefully so that, over time, the houses blend in with the landscape. These materials — corrugated iron, timber, fibro — also reflect our increasing desire to forge our own distinctly Australian style, as well as exhibiting a developing

regionalism, a response to both climate and environs.

And only now is urban architecture finally catching up. As the pressures of modern urban life increase, we yearn for the simplicity and carefree attitude that is embodied in the beach house which is why contemporary city homes now include many of the features previously only found in beach houses. Open-plan living areas; a blurring of the distinction between indoors and outdoors; free and easy access for ventilation; a welcoming-in of light but means of shielding rooms from the heat and glare of the summer sun; and features which address issues of privacy are all now a matter of course in architect-designed urban dwellings.

However, it is the architecture of holiday houses — both beach and country — that continues to lead the way. As Australians become increasingly sophisticated in matters of design, learning to appreciate that good design adds value, clients, as well as designers and architects, are taking more risks. We sanction, even encourage, innovative designs for beach houses because at the beach we are less likely to be concerned with impressing other people and with conformity. Just as we strip off on the beach regardless of our body size and shape, we allow our holiday houses to honestly express the identity of their inhabitants and their surroundings.

The town house is our public face — how we want to be seen by others; the beach house is an expression of how we really see ourselves.

The early beach houses

FISHERMEN'S SHACKS,
boathouses & fibro cottages

Anyone of his generation would know what he wanted. No transplanted bourgeoisie surburban brick-and-tile villa would do. The spirit of the shack had to be right, its character set preferably somewhere in the 1950s. It would need a properly casual, even run-down, beach air. It should have a veranda to sleep weekend guests, a working septic system, an open fireplace and somewhere to hang a dartboard. A glimpse at least of the Pacific through the trees was mandatory . . .

On a sunny spring day with a big swell running from the ocean straight into Broken Bay, he eventually found the shack he wanted . . . It was built of weatherboard and fibro-cement, painted the colour of pale clay, and it settled on the hillside sheltered from the southerly wind and facing north along the beach.

ROBERT DREWE, 'THE BODYSURFERS'

Long before the advent of the car, fishermen rowed into deserted little coves and pitched camp at certain times of the year when the fishing was good. Later more permanent dwellings built out of secondhand building materials appeared, providing shelter and a modicum of comfort against inclement weather. These shacks — some little more than boat or storage sheds — were probably the earliest form of beach houses.

As cars became more affordable and widespread they allowed people to head off along the coast, exploring the little fishing villages along the way, as well as venturing off the beaten track in search of their own Edens. They, too, built small storage sheds to house the trappings of summer holidays — tents, fishing rods, tools, etc. — which were gradually replaced by more and more substantial dwellings. And so the tradition of the beach house was born.

In parts of Queensland, disused farm buildings such as shearers quarters were trucked down from the hinterland to the coast to serve a new purpose as holiday houses. It was an early example of adaptive reuse and some of these original buildings can still be found in places like the seaside Queensland townships of Noosaville and Woodgate.

Ingenuity is a much lauded Australian trait, and it played a major part in the refurbishment of existing buildings into beach houses, as well as the erection of new purpose-built dwellings. These early beach houses — many built by completely unskilled hands from secondhand or found materials — had a temporary, improvised nature about them which was part of their charm.

Then along came fibro, a product first imported from France and the UK, but later manufactured here in Australia (local production began in 1916) and so widely used that it has come to be thought of as an exclusively home-grown product. Its timing, just as the concept of weekenders became popular, was perfect and it naturally became the most popular building material for such dwellings.

Fibro, originally made from cement bonded with asbestos fibre, was cheap and easy to handle. With a small amount of carpentry skill and know-how a simple fibro dwelling could be erected within a few days. The ease with which the board could be cut and manipulated also encouraged a certain amount of creativity in design. As Charles Pickett notes in his book *The Fibro Frontier*, 'Its cheapness and ease of use allowed ordinary home owners to become architects and builders, to express their personality through their homes.'

Topped with a skillion roof that ran either front to back or one side to the other, these original and character-filled houses had a rakish air and were given names such as 'Sea Spray', 'Edgewater' and 'Bali Hi'. Timber battens or narrow strips of fibro covered the joins which encouraged experimentation with various colour schemes — the ribs being picked out in a colour which contrasted with that of the walls.

But despite their often colourful visage (which at times verged on the lurid), the size and form of these beach houses remained respectful to the landscape. They did not try to dominate or subjugate their environs. They were unpretentious buildings, partly because of cost but also simply because of the kind of houses they were and the culture of the people who built them.

Architect John Mainwaring believes this lack of arrogance in their nature was one of their most appealing characteristics. Looking back at the land from the sea during an early morning dip is a memory that most of us, including Mainwaring, cherish, and the way the houses nestled into the landscape was something that we all found pleasing and somehow comforting.

It was not until the avaricious 1970s and 80s that people lost sight of the landscape while making grandiose and ill-fitting architectural statements in materials entirely unsuited to life by the sea.

Fibro houses had other advantages. They were cheaper and easier to maintain than timber houses, and when the family outgrew them extra rooms could simply be tacked onto the house, wherever they were needed. However, there were disadvantages too, such as a lack of thermal insulation. Unlined, these simple fibro beach houses heated up very quickly during the day, but they also cooled down rapidly at night.

Around Australia the fibro houses of the 1950s share many common features, regardless of location. When not covered with a textured coating to make them look like another, more substantial building material they are simple, honest dwellings. But for those who delight in their quirky characteristics and appearance, the sad fact is that they are rapidly disappearing as the value of coastal land increases and poor planning and zoning decisions continue to be made.

The humble fibro house of the past has not yet reached the stage where it is appreciated for the utilitarian dwelling that it is. But it should be. The unique architectural style of such houses is representative of a simpler age that is bound up in our collective memories of the beach and is one of the reasons why it is so special. For many people, the fibro cottage remains the quintessential Australian beach house and an expression of Australian identity.

SEA
urchin

This simple shack of corrugated iron, *right,* overlooking a sheltered bay on South Australia's Yorke Peninsula, was once the seasonal home for cray fishermen who fished these waters. It now serves as a weekend retreat, and has been painted the same colour as the vegetation so that it blends into the scrubby shoreline. A pergola covered with dried tea-tree provides shelter from the sun.

The shack is decorated with objects found washed up on the sickle of sand that surrounds the edge of the bay. Dangling from a bed post is a simple hanging, *above,* made of driftwood and seashells.

A desk occupies one corner of the main room, *right.* Underfoot, a simple sisal mat covers the lino. Like all of the furniture, the desk, pinboard and bookshelves have been made from recycled timber and driftwood.

A handpainted plate and cluster of shells are displayed in the bow of a small dinghy, *above*, which has been stood on its stern and is used as a storage cupboard.

The kitchen, *opposite*, takes up one wall of the main room. Strings of shells hang from the ceiling, which has been lined with split bamboo blinds. Large clam shells stored on top of the cupboards are not just decorative, but double as serving dishes. Drifting clouds have been painted across the walls, cupboards and even camouflage the fridge.

An alcove in the main room, *right*, houses a Balinese-style platform bed. Grey planks with softened edges, washed up by the sea, form its base. Linen is stored in wicker baskets underneath, and a small cupboard beside the bed provides further storage. Through the wire screen door is a lean-to storage area, toilet and washroom.

A small bunk room, *below*, sleeps four in beds made of recycled timber by one of the owners. Reflected in the glass doors is a view of the bay and scrubby dune vegetation. *Right*: Shells, sea sponges, driftwood and pieces of coral decorate the frame of a mirror.

This weatherboard shack, *right*, with the suitably
nautical name 'Snapper Lodge', sits just above the
high-tide mark on Sydney's Pittwater. A handbuilt
pizza oven by the water's edge becomes the focal
point of long, leisurely weekend lunches.

TIDEMARK

An old lifebuoy hangs on a wall that has been painted with
Porter's turquoise milk paint, with a wash of 'Oyster White' milk
paint over the top. Stored overhead are a couple of surf skis,
while below a runabout lies ready for the next fishing trip.

The main L-shaped room of the shack, *below*, houses the kitchen, master bed and living area. Most of the furniture was picked up cheaply at auction, while the kitchen shelving was made using offcuts of duckboard. A separate guest room, *right*, was decorated with stencilled fish to match the bedlinen.

All the walls of the main room are painted with Porter's acquamarine distemper. A sisal mat covers the floor and a collection of fishing paraphernalia hangs on one wall above an original print by Charles Blackman. To save floor space, the television is mounted above a window.

love
LORNE

Life at the cottage slows down to holiday pace. During the day, canvas deck chairs invite recline and relaxation. At night, a drawer full of playing cards provides after-dinner games.

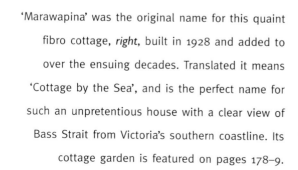

'Marawapina' was the original name for this quaint fibro cottage, *right*, built in 1928 and added to over the ensuing decades. Translated it means 'Cottage by the Sea', and is the perfect name for such an unpretentious house with a clear view of Bass Strait from Victoria's southern coastline. Its cottage garden is featured on pages 178–9.

When the current owners bought the cottage, they acquired not only the dwelling but all of its contents — from pieces of furniture such as the old kitchen dresser, *opposite*, right down to the crockery and cutlery, *left*.

The kitchen leads off the living room, *right*. The new owners have retained the original colour scheme both inside and out.

A bouquet of hebe blossom from the garden, *above*, decorates a table in the sunroom. *Above left*: a shell has been tied to the end of a lightcord to serve as a pull. The bathroom, *left*, with its pedestal basin, clawfoot bathtub and leadlight window, is completely authentic.

The fibro garage beside the front gate still has its original
pair of tongue-and-groove swinging doors, which have
been patched and painted many times over the years.

ART
house

One of the owners is an artist and teacher. Two of her recent gouaches on paper, *above*, are ready to be taken to the framers.

The origins of this tropical retreat on Queensland's Sunshine Coast are humble indeed. It began as a tractor-cum-tool shed which also served as a rough weekender. A year later, the owners decided to make it their permanent home. Floors were added, as well as two missing exterior walls, all of the interior walls, and a kitchen and bathroom. Most of the materials used in the construction of the house are recycled or home-made.

Every room in the house, including the living and dining room, *opposite*, is filled with art by contemporary Australian and New Zealand artists. Light floods this and other rooms through opaque corrugated polycarbonate panels in the roof, hidden behind canvas blinds. An old church pew provides bench seating along one side of the dining table.

Even the raked plywood ceiling in the master bedroom is hung with artwork. The bed is covered with a 1970s leather bedspread and a crocheted throw. Through the doorway is the bathroom, and an art-filled passageway beyond leading to a library and a laundry.

An old wooden ladder suspended above the kitchen sink, *right*, provides hanging space for various utensils. The concrete floor has been painted to resemble tiles. Standing at the sink one enjoys a view of the lagoon through the window, framed by a papaw tree and heavily laden passionfruit vine.

On one side of the bathroom, *below*, is a sunken bath which doubles as a shower recess. A full-length window behind the bath looks out onto a courtyard with a birdbath.

TREASURE chest

Many meals are taken on the terracotta tiled terrace, *right*, overlooking the water. The house is filled with a quirky collection of objects and furniture — such as the handpainted sign on the front door, *above* — which have been brought home from overseas trips or found at local shops and markets.

Sun filters through simple split cane blinds into the sitting room, *opposite*, of a 1930s fibro cottage which overlooks one of Sydney's northern beaches. A collection of storm shades are stored under a table ready to be carried out onto the terrace.

The dried fruit stem of a palm tree, *above*, makes a sculptural wall-hanging.

The kitchen, *opposite*, is much as it was when the owners moved in. They have given the cupboards a new coat of paint, painting over the ugly brown tiled splashback at the same time. Hanging above the kitchen table is a stash of baskets, along with a rope of garlic and a Balinese fish puppet. The handpainted and carved wooden boats on the wall were found in Greece.

Piled on the floor below a fishing net, *left*, is a rope hammock, left to lie there by the owners because they liked the shape it made. *Below*: A lamp covered in dried bamboo leaves casts a warm glow. Piles of books on every table indicate the contemplative nature of the house.

Opposite: Cushions covered in fabric found in Positano, Italy, are scattered over a four-poster bed. On either side of the bed, wide-bladed plantation shutters screen unattractive aluminium-framed windows from view.

Decorative
HOLIDAY
houses

Freedom to play

Each year, we rent a house at the edge of the sea and drive there

in the first of the summer arriving at a strange place a little before dark . . .

I never investigate the houses that we rent . . . all loom up in the last of the

sea light with the enormous appeal of the unknown. You get the sea-rusted

keys from the house next door. You unfasten the lock and step into a dark

or a light hallway, about to begin a vacation . . . But as strong as or

stronger than this pleasant sense of beginnings is the sense of having

stepped into the midst of someone else's life . . . I have never known the

people from whom we have rented, but their ability to leave behind them a

sense of physical and emotional presences is amazing.

JOHN CHEEVER, 'THE SEASIDE HOUSES'

Beach houses are all about letting go and being oneself. The same can be said about the process of decorating a beach house. They give us the chance to play, to create environments which just wouldn't work within the more formal constraints of a city dwelling where there is often the sense, real or imagined, that other people's expectations have to be met. At the beach there are no such constraints and we are free to create environments which reveal openly a side of our personalities that might otherwise be hidden from public view.

Being a secondary abode, where one slips into a more relaxed way of life, there isn't the need for lots of furniture or clutter —

the trappings of a busy city lifestyle. At the beach house less is definitely more and reinforces the notion of getting back to a simpler, more honest, existence which is part of the pleasure of escaping to the coast. Essential commodities are just one bed (or two, if the weekender is to be shared with family and friends), a large dining table and a number of chairs, a squashy sofa and perhaps some canvas deck chairs which can be dragged outside onto the verandah. And possibly also a hammock to string up under the trees.

Resist the temptation to fill the beach house with odd pieces of furniture which may have been in storage or cast-offs from well-meaning relatives. Unless there is some way to tie the whole scheme together (such as the use of a recurring colour), such an eclectic array of furniture styles will probably never gel. It can also be dispiriting to open a cupboard and find odd numbers of glasses and chipped dinnerware, frayed towels and mismatching sets of bedlinen. Furnishing a beach house need not be expensive and there should be absolutely no hurry to accumulate. Take time to comb local markets and homewares stores, selecting items carefully to ensure that they share a common design aesthetic.

Decorating a beach house can recall the same pleasures and delights that were to be had when embellishing one's first cubby or tree house. As then, items can be used for purposes other than those for which they were originally intended, for example silk saris draped over bedheads, dried palm fronds pinned to lampshades, and small shells tied to lightcords to serve as pulls. In the kitchen, large clam shells can be used as serving dishes; in the bathroom, smaller scallop shells can act as soap containers.

The casual nature of a beach house also creates opportunities for indulging in particular decorative fantasies and passions. Choose a theme — maritime, Moroccan, Mexican, whatever — and build upon it with every visit. (One of the joys of a beach house is that it can remain a perpetual work in progress.)

Beach houses encourage us to become more attuned to our natural surroundings, which is probably the reason why so many are decorated with objects found while beachcombing. Items such as palm husks, driftwood, shells and waterworn stones have intrinsic sculptural qualities that cannot be improved upon. Placed on tables or mantelpieces, or simply propped against walls in corners of rooms, such tactile items bring a little of the outside in, helping to reinforce the nature of the place.

As for colour, the strength of Australian light — especially by the sea — allows for a bolder palette than one might be tempted to use in the city. However, there are many good reasons for painting the outside of the house a colour that complements the surrounding vegetation or, if feasible, leaving the cladding untouched so that it eventually weathers, allowing the house to blend seamlessly into the landscape. Not only does this camouflaging effect create privacy, more importantly it respects the landscape in which the house is sited.

Inside, it's a different story. Here the desired mood of the house can dictate the colour scheme. If the beach house is to be a sanctuary from a stressed city existence, then softer, paler colours will create a suitably calming environment. Neutral spaces are the perfect backdrop where a view of an ever-changing ocean or wild bushland provides all the colour, texture and drama one could ever desire.

But if the beach house is to be a place for the unleashing of creative energies, stifled by the pressures of a nine-to-five occupation, then vibrant colours will suit the intended mood and encourage the creative spirit. Seek inspiration in the rich array of hues found in a shell or a peeling piece of bark.

Five of the houses in this chapter reflect the personalities of their owners (the sixth is a film set), and all contain elements of humour and fantasy. They are all highly decorated, with the architectural style of each house and sometimes its location influencing the form and style of decoration which has been continued throughout the interior. This has created a powerful sense of cohesion and integrity and, as a result, every room emits a feeling of purpose and well-being. Everything is in its right and proper place. Nothing is forced or ill-fitting.

Whilst five of the houses are perfect examples of complete harmony between owner and dwelling, the sixth is a vision of the perfect beach house. Together they are an idiosyncratic selection, as diverse as the people who created them.

high
TIDE

Like a mirage shimmering in the desert, this pavilion built on the rocky shores of Rottnest Island off the coast of Western Australia quickly vanished. Created as a set for an Australian feature film, *Under the Lighthouse Dancing*, the dream beach house designed by Larry Eastwood existed for eight short weeks before being dismantled and removed.

Stencils of stylised seaweed were punched out of the top of all four external walls, allowing for increased light and ventilation. The kitchen cupboards, *above*, were covered with perforated metal.

For the purposes of the film, the house had to face west for scenes shot at sunset. Louvred doors that could be folded back or slid out of the way allowed rooms to merge with the wide timber deck, *opposite,* which wrapped around three sides of the house. And there was a practical reason too: it made it easier to film in small rooms.

The house was built around a central enclosed garden. Dappled sunlight filtered into the living area, *above*, through a central pop-up roof, its shape inspired by Japanese pagodas. To simulate the colour and appearance of driftwood, a wash of diluted grey paint was applied to all of the furniture and the decking.

The film set had to combine every romantic notion about beach houses including open-plan living areas, a disinterest in privacy, and external walls that slid away to welcome in sea breezes and sunlight. Beside the house an outdoor shower, *opposite*, had a dress-circle view across the turquoise waters of Salmon Bay.

the CLIFF house

The Cliff House, *opposite*, is one of three self-contained beach houses available for lease which make up Hannafords, on Kangaroo Island off the coast of South Australia. Facing north and overlooking an azure Snellings Beach, *left* and *above*, it was built 30 years ago by the owners as their own family beach house.

An old brass light fitting adds a touch of Morocco to the interior.

A board documenting fishing catches made during the last 60 years gives guests some sense of the island's history.

The Cliff House was designed by its owners — an architect and an interior designer — and inspired by Mediterranean architecture. Local bricks were used, which were then lightly bagged and whitewashed both inside and outside. A curving stair from the sunroom, *opposite*, leads past a kitchen to one of the bedrooms, *above*, which fills the top of the tower and enjoys panoramic views of the ocean.

Norwegian
WOOD

About sixty years ago a Norwegian sea captain dismantled a log cabin in his homeland and reassembled it overlooking Pittwater, north of Sydney. A pool house, *right*, was built recently in the style and materials which echo that of the main house. Cedar shakes cover the roof and the exterior walls are clad in cedar boards, just like the main house where they were added to the exterior to provide extra insulation against weather. *Top right*: a couple of horseshoes for good luck are tucked behind a basket used to collect firewood.

The cabin was originally single storey, but the present owners have added another storey using logs from a dismantled portico. Panels of glass inserted into the roof, *left*, and continuing down the walls allow light to filter into the living room, *below*. The old wooden ceiling fan came from a picture theatre in Queensland.

A 'kitchen angel' made by a friend of the owners sits on a windowsill above the sink, *left*. The 1950s bowl of carrots was found in a junk shop in Bondi, while the painted carved fish over the window was bought in Palm Beach.

Chief, one of the owners' two Golden Retrievers, takes his place on the living room sofa, *left*. North American artefacts decorate the house. Both the American Indian rug over the back of the sofa and the carved figure wearing a feathered head-dress were bought in Montana, as was the cow skull, *above right*, hanging on a wall.

SUMMER
house

A private courtyard, *above*, outside the master bedroom provides a shady place to enjoy breakfast.

Designed a decade ago by Perth architect Louise St John Kennedy for a family with three teenage sons, this house, *right*, nestles into the bush facing Geographe Bay, *left*, in south-west Western Australia. Its brick veneer walls have been roughly trowelled with pigmented render the colour of sand which help it to blend into the landscape.

The house opens up on both sides to take advantage of cooling breezes. The conservatory leads into a dining room, with the kitchen to the left and a casual living area to the right. The floors are polished concrete for ease of maintenance, and feature a triangular motif which is repeated in the Y-shaped wrought-iron rods which decorate the French doors throughout the house.

Entry to the house is through the conservatory. The entire room is screened with timber lattice, backed with fine flywire screen. The room faces north, overlooking the tennis court in front of the house.

In the front garden, beside the tennis court, an outdoor shower, *above*,
provides somewhere to wash off the sand after a dip. Its lattice construction
and the surrounding tea-trees screen it and any occupant from view.

The master bedroom, *opposite*, opens onto its own private paved courtyard,
with views through the native garden down to an inlet. The plain materials —
dark timber furniture and French doors contrasted against the crisp white
bedlinen and canvas curtain — imbue the room with a sense of peace.

cape ESCAPE

Nautical objects, such as this pond yacht, *left*, decorate the house. Another model yacht, its sails blown away by strong winds, adorns the weather vane, *above*.

The cottage, *opposite*, stands in the grounds of 'Drik Drik' — a two-storey beach house on Victoria's Mornington Peninsula. Its name is Aboriginal for 'limestone', the main building material of both the house and the cottage. Italian stonemasons camped in the grounds for two years while building the house, using stone from a demolished lighthouse keeper's cottage. Although the house was finished in 1954, the secondhand materials used in its construction, along with the baronial style of the interiors, make it appear much older.

A large picture window at one end of the living room, *above*, frames the view of a multi-trunked eucalypt bearing a huge staghorn fern. Exposed stone walls and roof beams give the house's interior a European appearance.

During winter months owners and house guests congregate around a cast-iron stove, *right*, which burns constantly in a room off the kitchen.

A dining room leads off the large living room, *left*. On the floor flagstone borders surround sections paved with jarrah blocks which came from the old tram tracks in Melbourne, having long been replaced with concrete. The cast-iron stair balustrade is from the old members' stand at the Melbourne Cricket Ground.

Tucked away under the sloping roof of the main house is one of the guest rooms, *above*, decorated in pale pastels for female guests. A more masculine colour scheme decorates another guest bedroom.

An alabaster light fitting hangs in a guest bedroom on the first floor of the cottage, *opposite*. The bedhead was made to follow the line of the pitched ceiling. Glazed French doors open onto a small balcony.

ship to
SHORE

The large modernist house on a hill overlooking Scarborough Beach in Perth, Western Australia, has always been a landmark, but its new coat of vivid cobalt blue Boncote paint has gained it a certain degree of notoriety. Thought to have been built in the early 1950s by a concrete company, its design is an example of what is sometimes referred to as Inter-war Functionalist architecture, a style which had been popular in America. When the new owner chanced upon the house, it was in urgent need of repair.

Vivid colours are found inside the house as well as outside. The walls and ceiling of the living room, *left*, which was originally three separate rooms, are painted with vermillion signwriting paint. Twin portholes in the end wall frame circular views of a large aquarium behind. The floors throughout the house have been covered with plywood, varnished to a glossy shine.

An original speaker box still decorates the wall of the main staircase, *below*. The exterior balustrade, *right*, which trims the edge of the many decks and balconies, lending the house the appearance of an ocean-going liner, was carefully restored. The metal railings were painted with a special bronze enamel paint which gives them the appearance of hammered metal.

The master suite, *above*, with a gold ceiling and walls, opens onto its own balcony. A walk-in robe leads off to the right, and a bathroom fills one corner, tiled in dark green and gold glass mosaic tiles.

The kitchen was enlarged by incorporating what was originally adjacent servants quarters. A breakfast table now fills one corner of the orange room, *opposite*, which glows in the afternoon light. Because the ceilings, as well as the walls and floors, are concrete, trapeze lighting was the only viable lighting solution.

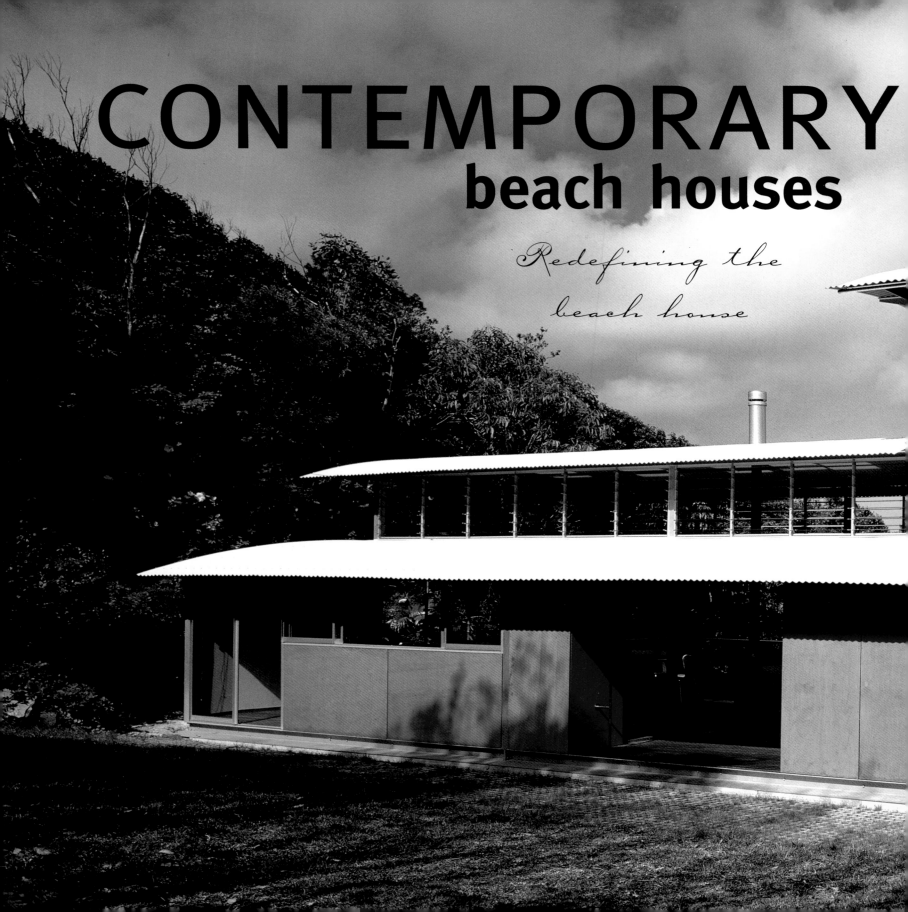

CONTEMPORARY
beach houses

Redefining the

beach house

eter . . . was an urban Australian who had turned his back on the bush and wholeheartedly embraced the coast, where as he often used to say, ninety per cent of the population lived anyway . . .

He had witnessed Australia's coming of age and was fiercely nationalistic, unfettered by any loyalty to old Europe. As an architect he designed houses that suited both his personality and the personality of his country. No cramped dark rooms or wasted space, just gracious lines of timber and tin, always with that all important 'view' in mind.

CANDIDA BAKER, 'SPINDRIFT'

If Australians are essentially a coastal people, then presumably the beach house — where we choose to spend our leisure time — is our favourite type of dwelling. It is interesting, therefore, to note that beach house architecture has always been more innovative than its urban counterpart.

There are many reasons for this. A lack of council conditions and restraints, as well as not having to impress or conform to neighbours and streetscapes, means that clients and architects alike have had the freedom to experiment and take risks, and in doing so, develop a distinctive architectural genre.

In the last couple of decades, as people have become more comfortable with the landscape and, at the same time, more concerned with environmental issues, beach houses have been designed to respond more directly to their setting, both in form and in materials. One of the reasons people head to the beach is to immerse themselves in nature and so it follows that they desire houses which open out to the surrounding landscape.

But not without restraint. Increased experience and knowledge of Australian climate and conditions means that people are more canny about ventilation and light, learning how to control what is let in and what is kept out in order to create comfortable living conditions all year round. Most of the houses in this chapter feature sheltered areas away from blustery onshore winds in the form of enclosed courtyards and decks to the lee side of the house. Most are also protected from the hot summer sun with wide eaves, pergolas or awnings, and although the latter also appear on city houses they owe much of their invention and increasingly sophisticated design to the beach house.

These, and other features of beach house architecture such as open-plan living spaces, a blurring between indoors and outdoors, a conscious regard for orientation and aspect, the need for adequate cross-ventilation and ease of maintenance are all now being incorporated into urban architecture.

And the reason is not just because such features suit our modern lifestyle and make for a more comfortable existence: it's that we want the essence of the beach house in our city homes. With the increasing pressures of modern urban life we crave privacy and sanctuary at day's end. What better way of

finding that than by borrowing salient features of beach house architecture which is synonomous with relaxed, casual living.

There has also been a rediscovery and increased use of what are generally considered to be local building materials. Corrugated iron and fibro cement board were used to clad beach houses long before making an appearance in cutting-edge urban architecture. These materials feature on the earliest examples of Australian vernacular architecture and so have a nationalistic appeal. As architects experiment with new ways to use these old products, leaving them unadorned so that they blend in with the surrounding landscape, a distinctively Australian form of architecture is emerging. Although containing many elements of past architectural styles, this new form of architecture is not simply revivalism: it's a synthesis of past styles and ideas which have worked.

The verandah, which wrapped itself around our earliest Australian colonial dwellings, is one element that's perfectly suited to beach house architecture. It provides somewhere to sit and meditate on the view and a sheltered place on which to entertain or dine. It also provides a breathing space between indoors and out, where one can briefly pause and assess the day before stepping into the full glare of the sun or downpour of rain.

Another feature of early homesteads which is being revived is the separation of various areas into different wings or pavilions. With changes in the structure of families, people require flexible accommodation. Beach houses are often shared by more than one group of people, so by separating sleeping areas from communal eating and living areas, important issues such as privacy and noise abatement are addressed.

Most of the houses in this chapter have been recognised as being particularly new or innovative by winning awards from bodies such as The Royal Australian Institute of Architects. They all include features we have come to expect in beach houses: generous open-plan living areas where the kitchen is central to the space; rooms that open directly to the outside; decks, verandahs or balconies big enough to dine out upon; innovative ways of shading windows and walls from direct sunlight; free and unimpeded cross-ventilation; and private sleeping quarters with ensuite bathrooms away from the communal areas of the house. All respond to their surroundings, having been orientated towards views of water, bushland or just simply garden.

This sensitive connection to the landscape in which the house is situated is perhaps the single most important feature of beach house architecture today, showing just how far we have come both realistically and in our imaginations towards fully understanding and possessing this place and so finally being at one with the land.

double
EXPOSURE

This timber house is one of two at Noosa Heads designed by architects Lindsay and Kerry Clare, which have been built on adjoining blocks of land — one directly behind the other — sharing only a narrow frontage to the road. An easement running alongside the beachfront house allows the second house direct visual and foot access to the beach, *right*. A series of decks at the front of the beachfront house, *inset*, are sheltered by pergolas and verandah overhangs.

The master bedroom, *above*, is tucked under a gracefully curved ceiling on a mezzanine level overlooking the living area. The bed, which incorporates bedside cabinets, was designed by the Clares.

Elements of natural climate control, such as high ceilings and walls of glass louvres, feature in the living room, *opposite*, of the beachfront house. Off to one side is a streamlined timber kitchen, *left*, which is flooded with natural light filtering down through a void. A curved island bench maximises space and facilitates movement through the area.

LATERAL
thinking

Sydney-based architect Tone Wheeler was commissioned to design a beach house on a tiny, remote island off the coast of Queensland for lateral thinker and writer Edward De Bono. The house had to be low-maintenance, ecologically responsible, flexible in layout and able to be locked up securely for long periods of time. A braced steel frame, which was prefabricated in Sydney and barged across to the island, elevates the house above the vegetation to catch cooling sea breezes. The exterior is clad in Symonite aluminium-faced panels.

Timber-framed doors slide completely out of the way, allowing the interior to merge with the decks. When the house is vacated, shutters are rolled down over the doors and panels slid over the windows, protecting the house from weather. The house is passively ventilated, with cooler air being drawn in under the eaves and out through louvres below the apex of the roof.

The view from the kitchen is out to sea. Appliances are kept to a minimum to save energy. Rainwater is collected from the roof and stored in tanks under the house for use inside. The interior of the house is clad throughout in plantation *Aracaria* (hoop pine) plywood.

The bedroom at one end of the house doubles as a writing room with a built-in desk along one wall under the window. The room opens onto its own deck, *opposite,* which runs across the full width of the house.

smooth
SAILING

Hidden behind the modern tallowwood decks rigged with
stainless-steel wire and trimmed with awnings, *opposite*,
is a solid brick bungalow. The original house did little to
capitalise on its view, *right*, across the sparkling, yacht-
strewn waters of Pittwater to Sydney's north, and so an
extension was added to the front of the house by architects
Kristin Utz and Duncan Sanby. The rejuvenated holiday
house has lured back both family and wildlife, *above*.

In the living room, *above*, an original 1940s fireplace was retained as a reminder of the house's history. The room has been substantially enlarged with the removal of two walls: one separating it from a small room near the front door, and another on the opposite side where two steps now lead down to a new dining area.

The view from one of the two new bedrooms, *right*, added to the front of the house, is reflected in its sliding glass doors. Both new bedrooms have ensuite bathrooms. Blue is used as an accent colour throughout the house, echoing the sea and sky.

As there are many dedicated cooks in the family, the kitchen, *opposite*, was moved to the front of the house where it is the hub of the new living area. Apart from being close to the view, it is now also immediately accessible to one of the front decks, *above*, on which many meals are taken.

FAR
pavilions

Architect John Mainwaring responded to the noisy site on which this Noosa house is situated by digging one side of it into a hill, creating an acoustic buffer between it and passing traffic. The house consists of four connected pavilions, each with a skillion roof. Clerestory windows of clear corrugated sheeting allow winter sun to penetrate the interiors.

Both the exterior and interior walls of the pavilions are clad in plywood, with exposed timber structural studs recalling the structure of old fishermen's houses. The central pavilion, *below*, comprises the living area and kitchen. The structural timber roof trusses are exposed, giving the interior a light, airy quality.

Two separate pavilions housing a bedroom and ensuite bathroom, *above*, are situated on either side of the central living pavilion. Each has an adjacent room of almost equal size which can be used as a studio, office or another bedroom. An old Morris 'Woody', *below*, owned by a local surfboard business passes by.

The kitchen is situated in one corner of the living area, underneath clerestory windows to take advantage of the natural light which streams in. Red ceramic tiles covering the splashback complement the rich colour of the jarrah benchtop and hardwood floorboards.

One side of the living area opens onto a west-facing verandah. A deep overhang provides shade from the hot afternoon sun. Sections of the exterior living room wall are filled in with timber louvres which allow constant cross-ventilation.

noble
SALVAGE

Late afternoon sun streams into the kitchen and living area, *above*, through glass doors which lead onto a wide cantilevered deck overlooking a beach and township on the south coast of New South Wales. Kitchen cabinets of silver ash veneer are divided by upright posts of brushbox. The island bench is topped with white granite.

The house presents a solid, weathered appearance, *right*, to the water. Its post-and-beam frame is constructed from massive old bridge timbers and recycled floor joists from woolstores, infilled with weatherboards of stringybark. Architect Clinton Murray's aim was to design a building which grounded itself as a wharf does, steadfast in the face of savage southerly busters.

The central hallway, *above*, runs from the front door past the
pool courtyard, *opposite*, terminating in the kitchen, dining and
living area. The house is shaped like a U, enclosing the
courtyard which provides a protected outdoor living space.
One arm of the house is two-storey, with a generous master
suite directly above the open-plan living area. A guest room
and ensuite are tucked behind the living area, with all other
bedrooms at the front of the house.

The master suite, *right,* comprises a large bedroom with a sitting area, separate dressing room and ensuite bathroom, *above*. The vanity and mirror frame are in stained American oak and the shower recess is lined with Carrara marble. A sandstone fireplace is centred on the exposed stone wall at the far end of the bedroom area, and a ledged and braced door leads out onto a private cantilevered balcony.

COAST
watch

While the front of this east-facing beach house designed by Ed Lippmann is all glass, the rear has been clad with plywood panelling, *right*, attached to steel stud framing. The curved roof is split into three sections, allowing for the insertion of a bank of clerestory louvres which draw cool air through the house.

Steel stacking doors slide out of the way so that the deck, which runs along the front of the house, *below*, becomes an extension of the living space. Because the site, on the south coast of New South Wales, is prone to high rainfall and unstable soils, the steel-framed house rests on six concrete piers which go down to a depth of six metres.

The living area rises to a height of one and a half storeys. At the southern end of the house is a two-storey wing, comprising two bedrooms and a bathroom on ground level and a master suite (bedroom, bathroom and study) above.

Slick finishes, such as a stainless-steel bench top, feature in the kitchen which is situated at the rear of the living area under a separate section of curved roof.

TERRA
firma

The owners of this house, *right*, which overlooks Bass Strait asked architect Kerstin Thompson for a house that would be 'rock solid'. Thompson responded by designing a house which mimicks the rockshelf edging the water. She chose to build the house in bricks and concrete blocks which were then covered with a blue-grey pigmented render, *below*.

The house is entered through the rear west-facing courtyard, *above*, which is sheltered from prevailing onshore winds and acts as a suntrap. Glass doors on both sides of the house mean that the sea is ever-present.

A freestanding moulded concrete step looking rather like an armchair sits under a doorway leading into a casual living area at the rear of the house. Full-length windows and doors to the north and west allow sun to stream into the room.

The master bedroom can be glimpsed through a doorway at one end of the generous, L-shaped, open-plan living area, *right*, while at the opposite end is a dining table and chairs, *below*. Behind the table a large oil painting is framed in a recessed section of wall and illuminated by its own narrow skylight.

The calming influence of a statue of Buddha flanked by lavender
bushes in the courtyard, *opposite*, seems to permeate an all-white
bedroom, *above*, with views over tea-tree to an ever-changing sea.

in PERSPECTIVE

Two distinct pavilions, linked by a rear concrete wall and a timber deck, comprise this house which lies between a rocky escarpment and the sea, about an hour's drive south of Sydney. The first pavilion encountered from the street, *below*, houses a large living area. The architect, James Grose, built the house into the landscape, *opposite top right*. Its angled roof allows winter sun to penetrate the house, but shields the rooms from the higher summer sun.

The construction of the house was simple: a concrete slab was poured for the floor, and included the built-in kitchen bench, *below*, and the back wall. The ceilings are lined with Zincalume mini-orb and the house has a steel frame. A horizontal display niche runs along the top of the rear wall of the living area, *left*. In winter the house is warmed by trapped heat radiating from this wall, topped up on cold nights by a coal-burning fire.

The rocky escarpment above the house forms a dramatic backdrop to the bedroom wing, viewed from the deck or from the living area. The bedroom wing can only be reached by going outside, which was something the owner insisted upon to remind occupants of where they were.

On winter days sunlight floods into the master bedroom through north-facing louvred windows. Built-in bookshelves behind the bed are one of the few examples of interior fittings within the house — which is in line with the owner's request for a very basic, functional house which utilised industrial materials.

OUT
in the OPEN

It's known as the Surf Beach House and it stands isolated in a dramatic setting on Victoria's Phillip Island. Designed essentially as a simple two-storey box measuring six metres square, Maddison Architects extended various elements such as decks, window frames and awnings in order to break up its cubic volume.

A balcony, which wraps midway around the house on three sides, offers panoramic views of the island and ocean, with even greater views being afforded from the roof-top deck. Solid balustrades provide some protection from strong winds, while battens in front of the windows shield the house from the western sun. The house is clad in compressed cement sheeting which has been left unpainted.

A spiral staircase links the ground and first floor, and continues on up to the roof deck. A guest bedroom, bathroom and laundry are on the ground floor, with the kitchen, main bed and living area incorporated into one room, *above and right,* on the first floor. Built-in storage minimises the need for excess freestanding furniture. Windows and doors have double seals as protection from weather on the exposed site.

between two WORLDS

The house, designed by Kerry Hill Architects and situated in the south-western corner of Western Australia, consists of two parallel pavilions — one for living, the other for sleeping — separated by a corridor and enclosing a sunny, sheltered pool court between them. The front living pavilion is a transparent box of steel and glass; the rear is of solid rammed earth and timber.

A pair of Alvar Aalto armchairs, *right*, sit in the living room end of the open-plan living and dining area at the front of the house.

The kitchen, *right*, has been reduced to its simplest form: a box-like island bench of pale terrazzo and stainless steel, with a bank of doors behind it housing a wall oven and concealing a pantry and fridge.

The completely glazed front facade of the living pavilion
faces north across paddocks of golden grass to distant
trees which shield glimpses of the Indian Ocean.

A narrow lap pool tiled in chocolate bronze glass mosaic tiles fills the small, glassed-in courtyard at the heart of the house. Behind it a corridor runs lengthways between the front and rear pavilions, and acts as a breezeway during temperate weather.

The guest bedroom, *left*, and an ensuite bathroom, *opposite*, are housed in a separate pavilion that stands apart from the main house, thus maintaining the privacy of both visitors and the owners. The rammed earth walls, a feature of the local architecture, provide shelter from cold south-westerlies.

All of the bathrooms feature the same restrained palette of colours and materials: clean white fittings, satin chrome tapware, pale terrazzo, offwhite mosaic tiles, polished concrete floors. Throughout the bedroom pavilion, small square windows set at varying heights depending on location, frame views of the surrounding landscape.

lightness of BEING

The interior of the house is as slick as the exterior. The kitchen, *above*, faces the dining and living areas. A tall bench hides kitchen clutter from view. Behind the kitchen is a bathroom and the bedroom.

The steel frame of this house, designed by Craig Rosevear, was precut, drilled and galvanised before being delivered to the site (near Hobart) and erected in just four days. Its prefabricated nature and its design on stilts above the ground is in deference to the fragile site, which is in a coastal protection zone.

The client's brief was for an open-plan, minimalist house with views from all major spaces.

He also asked to be shielded as little as possible from the external environment. At both

ends of the house, the floor and roof continue beyond the rooms to create covered decks.

The architect also designed the one bed in the house: a steel platform
which is bracketed to the wall and cantilevered into the room. The
bedroom and its deck face bushland, with Pipe Lagoon in the distance.

FORTRESS
mentality

The severe architecture of Barrie Marshall's own family beach house on Phillip Island, Victoria, is completely integrated into the windswept landscape in which it is sited. It hunkers down into the dunes, almost completely camouflaged from view. Built entirely in black pigmented concrete and galvanised steel, the house — just one room and a corridor wide — is entered via a large walled courtyard. A screen of steel jutting out into the courtyard, *above*, indicates the position of the front door.

The stainless-steel kitchen and dining area, *above*, look out across a colonaded terrace to the beach. The floors throughout the house are polished, black terrazzo.

An unexpected view of the interior and the sea beyond the house, *opposite*, is glimpsed through a window facing the courtyard. Brightly coloured horse blankets thrown over sofas and armchairs contrast with the relative austerity of the house's exterior and interior finishes. Native vegetation grows on the roof of the house, leading to the impression that it is buried in the dunes.

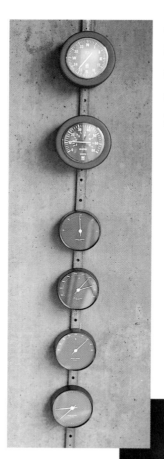

A series of instruments, *left*, hang in the corridor allowing occupants to judge the mood of the weather before they step outside.

Pivoting steel doors separate rooms along the length of the corridor, *right*. The entrance leads directly into the dining room and kitchen, with the living room beyond. Turning the other way, the corridor passes a laundry, two bedrooms and a bathroom, and ends in the master bedroom which has its own strikingly simple ensuite bathroom, *top right*. Small windows at floor level illuminate the passageway.

A tall, angled piece of steel creates a sharply futuristic bedhead for the custom-made bed in the master bedroom. Windows on one side of the room look out onto the beach and sea below the house, and on the other to the grassy, protected forecourt.

UP CLOSE
& practical
Detailing the beach house

...behind them, facing the sea [was] a scattering of surburban houses

straight from the middle-class outskirts of any western city in the world . . .

the range of architectural styles was unusually extreme, even impressive, in its

randomness and unfittingness to the arid environment and climate: mock-Tudor nestled

hard up against Mediterranean villa, then came three or four bleak, windswept blocks

dotted with FOR SALE signs, a Cape Cod or two, some ranch-modern experiments,

and an Australian-Romanesque edifice. They did, however, have some features in

common. . . a sprinkler whirred in each front garden; there were no fences but walls

had been cleverly erected to shield the grass and the cars from the sea breeze.

ROBERT DREWE, 'THE BODYSURFERS'

There was a time, not too many years ago, when most people preferred their houses to be as neat as a pin, shiny and pristine. Because the built environment in this country was (and still is) not very old, examples of buildings ageing gracefully were scarce.

But with more Australians travelling and becomingly increasingly sophisticated about design matters, we are at last appreciating the concept of patina, and the richness and depth it gives to our houses. This appreciation is also due to the widespread rise of the green movement, both nationally and globally, and a shift in the collective consciousness towards the environment that's affecting all areas of design, art and fashion. The gloss and polish of early decades is now regarded as a crass, two-dimensional veneer. Instead, the honest, unadorned qualities of natural materials that change and soften as they gracefully age and weather are sought after.

With resources becoming scarce, using recycled materials is becoming a moral imperative. Timber is now one of the scarcest commodities, and large pieces of it generally have to be salvaged from old industrial buildings or wharves. Such seasoned timbers give buildings strength of character and an instant patina, helping them to settle quickly into the landscape. But beach houses have had a long history of being more ecologically sound than their urban counterparts as many of the earliest were built using secondhand materials, while others — refurbished buildings such as boathouses and farm sheds — were examples of adaptive reuse long before the term was invented.

At the same time there has been a rediscovery of older materials which are regarded by most as our own. Corrugated iron and fibro cement sheeting have enjoyed such long and widespread use in this country that both have nostalgic and nationalistic qualities which lend the houses on which they are used a peculiarly Australian character.

However, these materials are now being used in new ways which gives them fresh appeal. Corrugated iron often clads walls (both external and internal), as well as roofs. Its ability to be bent and rolled has allowed architects and builders of beach houses in particular to experiment with curved and rolling roof forms that imitate the line of a wave poised to break or the wind-carved curve of a sand dune. Sometimes the roof forms are more angular, mimicking the shape of coastal vegetation sheared into strong diagonals by incessant onshore winds.

Fibro is now usually left unpainted. No longer containing health-damaging asbestos but made instead of sand, cement and cellulose fibres, fibro is again popular for the same reasons it was when first introduced: it is cheap, easy to cut and allows the designer great freedom and ease in cladding large expanses.

Being cost-effective also means that larger houses can be built using fibro for the same money as a smaller house in another material, or the savings can be channelled into other elements, such as fixtures and fittings.

But its popularity is not just one of cost. It is durable and attractive and some architects have made it their trademark. In fact, its appearance on cutting-edge beach house architecture has made fibro fashionable once more and it is steadily regaining its position as a viable, utilitarian building material that is not without aesthetic appeal.

The materials of a beach house built today are likely to include fibro, metal (corrugated iron, copper or stainless steel), glass and timber (reclaimed hardwoods, as well as marine-grade ply). There are regional variations based mainly on climate and local conditions, as well availability and historical precedents. In hotter, humid areas, lighter materials such as corrugated iron and plywood are likely to feature. So, too, will louvred windows, wide verandahs or external awnings to shade walls and windows, and glazed walls that slide or fold completely out of the way to allow the free flow of cooling breezes. Houses built in the tropics are also likely to be situated where they can catch such breezes, on hillsides or up off the ground on stilts — a lesson learned from the old timber Queenslanders which touched the earth ever so lightly.

As you travel south, materials become heavier and ways of sheltering houses from stiff onshore breezes are important to ensure year-round comfort for the inhabitants. Here houses are more likely to be built close to the ground, hunkering behind dunes or vegetation for protection, with internal courtyards which act as suntraps. However, the influence of tropical beach-house architecture has been the most pervasive and houses featuring large areas of timber and lattice, as well as similiar roof forms, are also found in southern states (as well as in the cities).

All around the country maritime influences prevail in beach house architecture, both in materials chosen as well as the design of methods used to shade outdoor areas from harsh summer sun. Marine-grade stainless-steel cable is often strung up as balustrade railings or pergolas over which to train creepers, as well as harnessing sail-shaped canvas awnings which float above terraces and decks, courtyards and balconies.

Such indoor-outdoor spaces are crucial to beach house architecture: a beach house is simply not complete without a place that's neither inside nor outside but linked to both, providing protection from the elements without inhibiting seabreezes and sunlight.

WINDOW
treatments

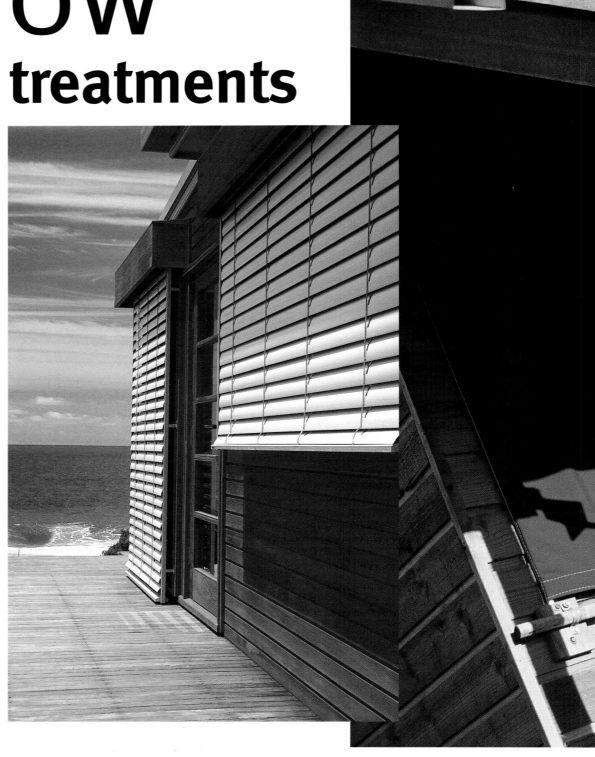

Shading the outside of a window from direct sunlight will keep a house cooler than just using internal blinds. Exterior metal venetian blinds, *right*, are one way of doing this. Fixed rails on either side of the window keep the blinds firmly in place.

At Eco Beach Resort near Broome, on the north-west coast of Western Australia, cabin windows are fitted with canvas tarpaulins, *far right*, in place of glass. Deep eaves shade the windows from the hot sun.

In the living room of a house on Stradbroke Island, off the coast of Queensland, architects Brit Andresen and Peter O'Gorman have used corrugated opaque fibreglass for the exterior wall, *opposite*, overlaid with horizontal rows of narrow hardwood battens both inside and outside which cast contrasting shadows.

Three window treatments feature in the living room, *above*, of a house designed by Utz-Sanby. Motorised metal louvres above the glass roof limit the amount of direct sunlight, with louvres below permitting sea breezes. Timber planks fixed on an angle outside the end window give privacy without blocking the view.

Deepwater Point Pearl Farm outside Broome is built in the style of architecture which is peculiar to the region. Because of extreme heat and also the possiblity of cyclones, timber awnings shading each window can be propped out on struts while the weather is calm, or battened into place when a cyclone hits.

Double-hung windows without horizontal rails allow occupants an uninterrupted vista over a township on the south coast of New South Wales, from a house designed by architect Clinton Murray. The south-west facing windows are tinted to prevent glare and reduce heat.

On this West Australian house, designed by Kerry Hill, hinged screens of horizontal timber battens have been fixed to the exterior of north- and west-facing windows. The angle of the battens prevents summer sun from entering the master bedroom, while not inhibiting the view.

AWNINGS
& sun shades

Canvas awnings laced onto a galvanised steel frame, *right*, shade the wrap-around deck of the beach house film set featured on pages 44–49. Seaweed-like stencils above louvred doors and windows allow constant ventilation.

Architect James Grose of Bligh Voller Nield has diffused the amount of sunlight striking this house, *right*, at Whale Beach, New South Wales, with simple awnings of untrimmed bamboo rods wired to steel frames. External metal venetian blinds cover a north-facing window.

A retractable canvas awning provides dappled shade over the timber deck of a house designed by Tone Wheeler at Pearl Beach, New South Wales. The strips of canvas not only filter the sunlight, but allow breezes through. Adjustable metal louvres provide more solid shade where it is needed above sliding doors and windows.

Two sail-shaped canvas shadecloths cover an enclosed north-facing courtyard of a house on the central coast of New South Wales. The awnings are attached with stainless-steel cables to the house at one end and to a metal mast-like post which is braced to one wall at the other.

An awning, *above*, shading the balcony of a New South Wales central coast beach house designed by architect Rob Pullar is attached to poles welded onto the balustrade. Because of high winds, stainless-steel cables have been used to tension the awning to various points in the garden.

A triangular canvas awning shades the entrance to a house, *opposite*, situated on the water at Flinders, Victoria. North-facing clerestory windows are shaded by external metal venetian blinds.

DECKS
& verandahs

Twin balconies are cantilevered off the front of a two-storey beach house, *below*, designed by Clinton Murray. The view from the uppermost deck, *right*, is panoramic. An angled window jutting out from the side wall extends the view to incorporate a distant mountain peak.

At one end of a Stradbroke Island house designed by Brit Andresen and Peter O'Gorman, *right*, are two decks: the top with a pitched roof and woven hardwood balustrades affords water views; the lower one is simply a platform suspended above the scrubby vegetation.

Old red gum railway sleepers laid parallel create a wharf-like front terrace outside the shack featured on pages 14–19. The terrace is sheltered by a pergola of tea-tree brush supported by forked tree trunks. Thick sailors rope looped around posts makes a suitably nautical balustrade.

Much of the balustrade on the balcony which wraps around three sides of the
Phillip Island house featured on pages 118–121 is infilled with panels of unpainted
compressed cement board to protect occupants from the wind. Steel angles
forming the balustrade's uprights have been left to jut below the level of the deck.

Cantilevered decks, *right*, hang off the front of the Clinton Murray-designed house featured on pages 98–103. At night the facade of the house, as well as the balustrades of recycled timber and stainless-steel cables, are thrown into sharp relief by Kreon lights embedded in the deck, *below*.

Adjacent to the kitchen of the Kerry Hill-designed house featured on pages 122–127 is a sheltered north-east facing deck, just right for peaceful breakfasts. It is enclosed by a wall of rammed earth and timber which provides shelter from cold southerly winds.

As in most houses built in north-west Western Australia, the enclosed verandah of Deepwater Point Pearl Farm, north of Broome, is used as living space and wraps around internal bedrooms. Corrugated iron is used to clad walls as well as ceilings, and jarrah boards line the floors.

EXTERIOR
materials

The severe street-facing facade, *below*, of the house featured on pages 98–103, is relieved by two chimney cowls peeping over the roof and, when the front double doors are opened, a glimpse of the sea through the house. The recessed entrance is framed by massive old salvaged timbers, *top left*, infilled with stringybark weatherboards.

In the sheltered front courtyard of a house designed by Clinton Murray, *below*, the decking timbers continue up the front wall of the house, and the courtyard is surrounded by a tall fence made of narrow hardwood sticks used in the local oyster industry.

Architect Robert Riddel originally designed this fibro-clad beach house on Stradbroke Island, Queensland, as an extension to a 1950s house next door. It was later converted into a separate dwelling. The triangular balcony juts out from the front of the building like the prow of a ship. A tall, curved balustrade of timber battens on one side provides privacy and shade, and directs one's gaze towards the view to the east.

Opposite: A range of materials clad the exterior of a house designed by Kerry and Lindsay Clare in Noosa, Queensland. The ground floor walls are rendered masonry, while the first floor walls are clad in weatherboard. Painted sheets of compressed fibre cement sheeting flank a screen of timber battens which hides an upstairs recessed window from view.

The tall tower wing, *left*, of a house designed by Queensland architects Donovan Hill captures distant ocean glimpses from Queensland's Stradbroke Island. It is clad in compressed cement sheets, separated by vertical hardwood battens. A rooftop deck cantilevered out over a window acts as an awning.

Below: John Mainwaring chose plywood as the exterior material for the house featured on pages 94–97, with the connecting passageways between the four pavilions clad in corrugated Zincalume.

The walls of the rear section of the twin-pavilioned house featured on pages 122–127 are built of rammed earth — a building material which is popular in the south-west of Western Australia where this house is situated. They provide a textural contrast to the front pavilion of glass and steel, and an almost blank facade to the nearby road.

The masonry block walls of the house designed by Kerstin Thompson, featured on pages 108–113, are rendered with pigmented concrete, *right*. The colour of the walls changes from blue-grey to smoky purple depending on the light conditions and time of day.

A rusting metal plate fronts an elemental letterbox for the house featured on pages 114–117. Five horizontal ribs detail the top edge of the wall, which runs right through the house, forming its rear wall. The large brackets support one side of the raked roof.

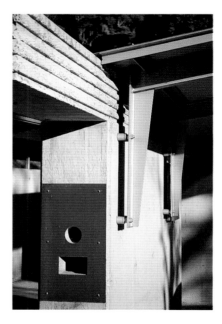

seaside
GARDENS

Working with nature

love this house . . . white timber with window-walls, the house looks out into the jungle. I love this sloping, hillside, garden where rough, boisterous bush fairies run amok, a forest of ti-trees and wattle leaning against the fall of the land, matting and weaving ceilings of leaves, making crazy designs of sunlight on the earth beneath. Wild place . . . You cannot see where it ends because lawn turns to ti-tree scrub, knotted limbs and clearings full of pale green leaves shaped like teardrops.

JOANNA MURRAY SMITH, *TRUCE*

A seaside garden is perhaps the most challenging form of gardening there is. Here, within seaspray's distance of the pounding surf, plants have to cope with onshore, salt-laden winds and often unsustaining sandy or rocky soil. Attempting a surburban-style garden full of exotics in such conditions requires inordinate amounts of time and energy to keep it alive. And the end result usually looks out of place.

Consider instead a garden based on the natural vegetation of the area which has adapted to local conditions. The line between your garden and the land beyond the boundaries of your property will then dissolve, and the view down to the water, or across to distant cliff or into bush will be harmonious and uninterrupted.

This doesn't mean abandoning thoughts of a garden in the cultivated sense of the word, but building on what is there, adding to it with other species of plants which thrive in similar conditions. Such a garden is also relatively low-maintenance — an important consideration given that it will be left to look after itself much of the time.

Around any house there is always a variety of microclimates which suit different plants, but more particularly so by the sea. Depending on where the house is situated, the front garden may take the full brunt of the weather, while the garden behind the house lies sheltered from the wind. There may be courtyards which act as suntraps, baking even the most hardy of flora, or narrow, draughty passageways which remain in solid shade for most of the day. Each of these areas calls for a different approach and different species.

Beach houses are often unusual and unique in their architecture, and the gardens surrounding them can be equally bold, reflecting the style of the house. Plants can be chosen which emphasise certain architectural features such as colour and form. Many species that thrive in harsh environments are inherently quite sculptural, and others become so as onshore winds shear them into spectacular shapes.

Any kind of seaside garden — natural or exotic — benefits if the soil is improved and the wind screened to lessen its impact. Sandy soil drains too quickly for most plants to take advantage of the moisture that briefly passes through it. To increase its water-holding capacity, organic material such as compost can be dug through it and then a thick layer of bark, straw, leaf litter or even seaweed can be heaped upon its surface to trap the moisture and reduce weed growth. Eventually this mulch will break down, adding much needed nutrients to the soil and another layer will have to be added.

The wind can be screened in a few ways. Even a slight rise or dune shields a seaside garden from the worst of its force. In its absence (or to increase its height and therefore its effectiveness) a row of hardy, highly salt-tolerant shrubs can be planted along the boundary. This hedge will become the front line for the rest of the garden, providing shelter behind for species which are less tolerant to wind and salt. A solid fence won't work as well because of the turbulence it causes as wind gusts whirl over the top, flattening whatever is growing behind. And, besides, who wants a fence between them and the view?

When deciding what to plant, resist species which spread quickly into bushland. Those with colourful berries, such as cotoneaster and Mickey Mouse plant (*Ochna serrulata*), spread effortlessly. Others which have become a nuisance include privet, lantana (though not the garden variety), morning glory, buddleia, *rhaphiolepsis*, canna lilies, nasturtiums, Italian lavender, freesias, cassia, coreopsis and some species of broom.

Native plants attract wildlife and so help to preserve some of the delicate ecosystems that are rapidly disappearing as coastal vegetation is cleared for housing. Blossoms dripping with nectar lure insects and birds to feast on the bounty and the garden will soon fill with colour and movement as small birds dart in and out of bushes in search of sweet nectar or fluttering insects.

Consider, too, the need for shade in the garden. Trees that shade windows and walls from the hot summer sun keep the house cooler inside, as well as providing shelter for smaller, shade-loving plants and also a place to string up a hammock.

Materials chosen for hard landscaping (retaining walls, decks, paths and steps) should be those which age and weather well, requiring little maintenance. Timber and stone settle quickly into a garden, adding another quality.

The garden will continue to give pleasure well beyond sunset and remain a useable space if it is lit at night. With the scent of drying grass and fragrant flowering plants such as frangipani in the air, and the murmur of the sea in the background, the garden is full of sensory pleasures after dark. Low-voltage halogens are the most permanent and professional way to light a garden, but simple bamboo flares and outdoor lanterns can transform it, altering its dimensions and imbuing it with magical qualities so that you experience it anew.

The garden is, after all, not just the space around the house that you walk through on the way to and from the beach. It is another 'room' to be lived in and enjoyed — an intrinsic part of the beach house and our memories of it.

SEAFRONT
garden

Israel grass helps to bind the fragile dunes together, *right*, at Callala Beach, New South Wales. On Kangaroo Island, off the coast of South Australia, coast rosemary, native grasses, succulents and saltbush, *below*, create a tapestry of colour and texture amongst the rocks.

Carpobrotus aequilaterus, below, a spreading succulent, is often found growing on sand dunes.

Apart from the Israel grass which covers the dunes at Callala Beach, there are clumps of introduced bitou bush as well as exotics including aloe, African daisies, freesias, nasturtiums and hardy pelargoniums which have all seeded from people's gardens.

SUCCULENT garden

A Mediterranean-style house at Pearl Beach, New South Wales, *opposite*, is surrounded by aloe and yucca, with a carpet of self-sown yellow gazanias.

Below: Growing beside a fibro boat house at Maianbar, New South Wales, is a handsome stand of *Agave attenutata,* and a large, mature *Euphorbia*.

Clockwise from below: Aloe arborescens; Echeveria elegans; a spotted aloe hybrid. Because succulents don't require much attention, they make good pot plants.

Mediterranean
GARDEN

A profusion of flowering plants creates a meadow-like effect, *below*, in a garden overlooking the sea. Calendula and daisies are intermingled with flowering borage and aniseed.

In a coastal garden overlooking Whale Beach, New South Wales, *opposite*, a clump of *Echium candicans*, or Pride of Madeira, grows near a stand of indigenous casuarinas. The rich purple blooms, *above*, attract bees. Another hardy blue-flowering plant for seaside gardens is *Eryngium, top left,* commonly called sea holly.

COTTAGE
garden

Agapanthus, hebe and saltbush peep through the fence, *below*. A hedge of tall tea-tree screens the cottage from view and arches over the original wire mesh gate. In front of the fence, a profusion of yellow gazanias and pink pelargoniums fill the nature strip.

Among flowering plants which can tolerate salty conditions are *Hemerocallis* (day lilies), *below*.

Sheltered by the tall front hedge, the side garden, *opposite*, of the cottage featured on pages 24–29 includes a *Camellia japonica*, as well as hebe, a Tom Thumb fuchsia, lavender and shasta daisies.

TROPICAL
garden

One of the oldest houses in Darwin, *above*, on Myilly Point, overlooking
Fannie Bay, is surrounded by a grove of palms and ferns. The plaited
trunk of a mature palm, *top right*, provides textural interest at eye level.
Colourful bromeliads, *right,* need dappled light and warm conditions.

Hibiscus, such as this *Hibiscus rosa-sinensis* 'Jay's Orange', require shelter from strong winds. Blooms generally last no more than a couple of days, but providing the plant gets enough sunshine it will bloom profusely from late spring into autumn.

The leathery leaves of *Codiaeum variegatum* (commonly known as crotons) come in an amazing range of colours. They will not tolerate temperatures below 10 degrees Celcius and prefer partial shade and fertile, moist but well-drained soil. Tip prune to promote bushy growth.

Kniphofia are hardy plants and will tolerate reasonably harsh conditions, although they do require well-drained soil, kept moist in summer. The common name — red-hot poker — is a slight misnomer, as they flower in a range of colours: green, cream, yellow, orange and various shades of red.

Canna lilies are tall, handsome accent plants for the rear of garden beds. They are grown as much for their luxuriant foliage as for their brightly coloured flowers. They require a warm, sunny position and rich, moist soil. Remove seed heads to prevent them from spreading.

BUSH
garden

The owner of a house, *opposite*, designed by Jim Koopman near Sydney's Palm Beach is passionate about native flora and bush regeneration. His house is surrounded by tree ferns, eucalypts, acacias and angophoras. Old bark peeling from a native angophora, *right*, reveals the typical smooth reddish trunk beneath.

Epidendrum ibaguense, an epiphytic orchid, such as the one *below* draws all the moisture and nutrients it requires from the air. *Right: Xanthorrhoea australis* (grass trees or yaccas) appear throughout much of Australia. They are slow-growing but long-lived, requiring full sun and well-drained soil.

DETAILING
the garden

Beach houses are often perched on dunes or cliffs above the water and steps of some kind are necessary to access the beach. Timber is the most common material, whether it be new, *above* and *above right*, or old railway sleepers, *above left*. Even old concrete steps will do, such as those *left*, which have been softened by plantings on either side.

Stone steps lead down to the water, *opposite*, in a garden designed by Michael Cook on the central coast of New South Wales. The path is fringed with clivia on one side and native grass (*Carex*) on the other.

The letterbox, *above,* for The Cliff House on Kangaroo Island (featured on pages 50–53) is made from driftwood. *Left:* Andrew Murray adorned a flecked concrete pathway leading to a beach house with the imprint of a John Dory. The path runs alongside a well-mulched bed of *Banksia spinulosa* 'Birthday Candles'.

An outdoor shower, *left*, or at least a means to hose down one's feet, *far left*, are essential features of the seaside garden.

A low timber bench running the length of the deck, *below*, provides permanent seating, while also doubling as a balustrade.

Stepping stones lead past a concrete birdbath made by Andrew Murray, *right*, to the front gate of a house designed by Clinton Murray. The front fence is clad in narrow oyster sticks and the gate in panels of galvanised steel and Zincalume.

A rectangular pond, *above*, fills one end of the rear courtyard of the Kerstin Thompson-designed house featured on pages 108–113. The steel sculpture in the pond was made by Inge King. In another corner of the same courtyard, *top left*, is a terracotta urn.

Opposite: The rear, sheltered courtyard of a house designed by Utz–Sanby overlooking one of Sydney's northern beaches is paved in a chequerboard pattern to form a large chess board. Reaching the chess board requires stepping across a narrow pond.

plant list

The following list of plants will tolerate extreme conditions.

TREES: *Agonis flexuosa (peppermint tree/ willow myrtle); *Albizia lophantha (Cape Leeuwin wattle/silk tree); *Banksia integrifolia (coast banksia), B. serrata (old man banksia); *Casuarina equisetifolia (coast she-oak); *Cupaniopsis anacardioides (tuckeroo); *Eucalyptus cladocalyx (sugar gum), *E. diversifolia (South Australian coast mallee), *E. obliqua (messmate); *Hakea salicifolia (willow-leafed hakea); Harpephyllum caffrum (Kaffir plum); *Lagunaria patersonia (Norfolk Island Hibsicus); *Leptospermum laevigatum (coastal tea-tree); *Melaleuca; Metrosideros excelsa (New Zealand Christmas bush/Pohutukawa); olive; Pittosporum crassifolium (karo)

SHRUBS: *Acacia longifolia (Sydney coast wattle); Acokanthera oblongifolia (African wintersweet); *Brachysema celsianum (Swan River pea); *Calothamnus villosus (woolly net bush); *Correa alba (native fuchsia); *Dillwynia retorta (twisted parrot pea/egg and bacon plant); Echium candicans (Pride of Madeira); hebe; *Kunzea ambigua; leucadendron and protea species; Rhaphiolepis umbellata (Indian hawthorn); *Westringia fruticosa (coast rosemary); *Thryptomene saxicola (heath myrtle); yucca

PERENNIALS, GROUNDCOVERS, HERBS: aloe; Arctotis (African daisy); Agave; Artemsia (wormwood); Carpobrotus (sea pigface); Cerastium tomentosum (snow in summer); Cineraria maritima (dusty miller); Cistus (rock rose); echeveria; Eryngium (sea holly); gazania; Helichrysum splendidum; *Leucophyta brownii (cushion bush); many native grasses; pelargonium; Persicaria (Japanese knotweed); Phormium tenax (New Zealand flax); *Ptilotus (mulla mulla); Santolina chamaecyparissus (lavender cotton); Sedum; Limonium (statice/sea lavender); rosemary; Armeria maritima (thrift/sea pink); thyme; Wedelia trilobata; *Xanthorrhoea (grass tree/yacca)

CLIMBERS: bougainvillea; *Hardenbergia violacea (false sarsparilla); *Hibbertia scandens (guinea flower); Muehlenbeckia (lignum, wire vine); Solandra maxima (golden chalice vine)

* denotes natives

photography credits

Farshid Assassi: back cover, 76–77, 104–107

Reiner Blunck: 81, 82, 83 (bottom), 165

Jenna Reed Burns: endpapers, 5, 6, 7 (bottom left), 8, 9, 43, 138–139, 142, 143, 150, 151, 168–169, 171, 172 (bottom left and right), 174, 175 (top left and bottom left), 180, 181 (top right), 182 (bottom left and right), 184, 187

Leigh Clapp: 152, 175 (top right and bottom right), 176, 177, 178 (left), 181 (top left, bottom right and left), 185

James Grose: 149

Greg Holmes: 80, 83 (top)

Peter Hyatt: 114–117, 167 (bottom right)

Simon Kenny/Belle magazine: front cover, 3, 20–23, 44–49, 148

Lansdowne/Greg Barrett: 2, 34–39, 54–57, 182 (top right), 183

Lansdowne/Earl Carter: 1, 10–11, 13, 24–29, 64–69, 108–113, 132–137, 141, 153, 167 (top right), 178 (right), 179, 188 (left and bottom right)

Lansdowne/Darren Centofanti: 14–19, 50–53, 156–157, 186 (top right)

Lansdowne/Robert Frith: 7 (top left and bottom right), 40–41, 58–63, 70–75 (styled by Nerida Nicholas), 79, 122–127, 147, 160, 166

Lansdowne/Michael Hutchinson: 146 (left), 161

Lansdowne/David Sandison: 30–33, 94–97, 164 (bottom right)

Trevor Mein: 118–121, 144, 155, 158, 163, 164 (left)

Janusz Molinski: 7 (top right), 99, 101, 146 (right), 159, 162 (top left and bottom right), 186 (left)

Lorna Rose: 172 (top), 173

Eric Sierins: 88–93, 145, 189

Alison Taylor: 98, 100, 102, 103, 154, 162 (bottom left), 188 (top right)

Tim Wheeler: 84–87

Leigh Woolley: 128–131

acknowledgements

The author would like to acknowledge the generous assistance of the following people in the preparation of this book:

The owners of the various houses featured herein, including Jenny and Patrick Opie (Sea Urchin), Peter Lewis (Tidemark), the Watts family (Love Lorne), John and Lyn McCrea (Art House), Belinda Hannaford (The Cliff House), Nancy and Warwick Pilcher (Norwegian Wood), Libby and Vaughan Burt (Summer House) and Greg Barrett (Bush Garden).

All of the architects who kindly agreed to be included in this book, and particularly John Mainwaring for giving me his honest and straightforward account of beach house history and the evolution of its architecture.

The commissioned photographers for their evocative images.

And finally, Deborah Nixon for asking me to do this book, and Kate Merrifield for her unfailing good humour; Stella de Vulder for many good contacts; all at *Belle* for their interest and assistance; and Philip Reed and Chris Burns for their enthusiasm and support.

TEXT

Chapter 1: Extract from *The Bodysurfers* by Robert Drewe, reprinted by permission of Pan Macmillan Australia Pty Ltd. Copyright Robert Drewe, 1983.

Chapter 2: Extract from 'The Seaside Houses' by John Cheever. First published in *The Brigadier and the Golf Widow*, Victor Gollancz, London, 1965. Reprinted by permission of Aitken, Stone & Wylie Ltd on behalf of the Estate of John Cheever.

Chapter 3: Extract from *The Powerful Owl* by Candida Baker, reprinted by permission of Pan Macmillan Australia Pty Ltd. Copyright Candida Baker, 1994.

Chapter 4: Extract from *The Bodysurfers* by Robert Drewe, reprinted by permission of Pan Macmillan Australia Pty Ltd. Copyright Robert Drewe, 1983.

Chapter 5: Extract from *Truce* by Joanna Murray Smith, Penguin Books Australia, 1994. Copyright Joanna Murray Smith, 1994.

bibliography

Boyer, Marie-France, *Cabin Fever*, Thames & Hudson, 1993

Darblay, Jerome and D'Arnoux, Alexandra, *Seaside Houses*, Ebury Press, 1993

Drew, Philip, *The Coast Dwellers*, Penguin Books, 1994

Drewe, R. (ed.) *The Picador Book of the Beach*, Picador, 1995

Grow What Tree, Thomas Nelson, 1985

James, Theodore, *Seaside Gardening*, Harry N. Abrams, 1995

Jarratt, Jackie, *Noosa Style*, The Blue Group, 1998

Kreel, Fleur, 'A Shore Thing', *The Sydney Morning Herald*, 19 June 1997

Malouf, David, 1998 Boyer Lectures transcripts, *The Sydney Morning Herald*, October/November 1998

Monfries, Marcelle, *Seaside Gardening in Australia*, Methuen, 1987

Pickett, Charles, *The Fibro Frontier*, Powerhouse Publishing & Doubleday, 1997

Quarry, Neville, *Award-Winning Australian Architecture*, Craftsman House, 1997

Splash: Stories for Hot Summer Days, Penguin Books Australia, 1998

Taylor, Jennifer, *Australian Architecture Since 1960*, The Law Book Company, 1986

Welsh, John, *Modern House*, Phaidon Press Limited, 1995

Winton, Tim, *Land's Edge*, Picador, 1998

Woolley, Jim, *Abode of Our Dreaming*, USQ Press, 1997

index

(page numbers in italic type indicate photographs)